CHRISTMAS AT HOME

Homemade Christmas Sweets

Jennifer Hahn

BARBOUR BOOKS
An Imprint of Barbour Publishing, Inc.

© 2002 by Barbour Publishing, Inc.

ISBN 1-58660-548-8

Cover image © Getty One, Inc.

Published by Barbour Books, an imprint of Barbour Publishing, Inc., P.O. Box 719, Uhrichsville, Ohio 44683, www.barbourbooks.com

Member of the
Evangelical Christian
Publishers Association

Printed in Canada.

Contents

*"Then the King will say to those on his right,
'Come, you who are blessed by my Father;
take your inheritance, the kingdom prepared for you
since the creation of the world.
For I was hungry and you gave me something to eat. . . .'*

*"The King will reply, 'I tell you the truth,
whatever you did for one of the least of these brothers of mine,
you did for me.'"*

MATTHEW 25:34–35, 40

Bars and Squares

*"He has shown kindness by giving you rain
from heaven and crops in their seasons;
he provides you with plenty of food
and fills your hearts with joy."*

ACTS 14:17

Reese's Squares

2 sticks butter, melted
5 c confectioners' sugar
1 c semisweet chocolate chips

2½ c peanut butter
4 tbsp butter, melted

Mix 2 sticks melted butter and peanut butter until smooth. Add confectioners' sugar. Put into a 9x13-inch baking pan. Pat down firmly. Combine 4 tbsp melted butter and chocolate chips until smooth. Spread on top of peanut butter mixture. Refrigerate 2 hours. Cut into squares.

Chocolate Cherry Bars

1 pkg fudge cake mix
1 tsp almond extract

1 large can cherry pie filling
2 eggs, beaten

Combine all ingredients in a large bowl until well mixed. Spray 9x13-inch pan with cooking spray. Pour batter into pan and bake at 350° for 25–30 minutes. When cool, add frosting. Can also be served with whipped topping or ice cream.

Fudge Frosting:

1 c sugar   ⅓ c milk
5 tbsp butter or margarine   1 c chocolate chips

Combine sugar, butter, and milk in saucepan. Boil 1 minute, stirring constantly. Remove from heat and stir in chips until smooth. Let thicken slightly and pour over cooled bars.

Double-Chocolate Mud Bars

½ c butter, softened
1 c sugar
2 large eggs, separated
1½ c flour
1 tsp baking powder
½ tsp salt

1 c walnuts, chopped
½ c semisweet chocolate chips
1 c miniature marshmallows
1 c brown sugar, firmly packed
1 c M&M's (optional)

Beat together butter and sugar. Add egg yolks one at a time. In a different bowl, mix together flour, baking powder, and salt. Fold flour mixture into butter mixture. Press mixture into greased 9x13-inch baking pan. Pack down firmly. Sprinkle walnuts, chocolate chips, marshmallows, and M&M's over top of mixture in pan.

Beat egg whites at high speed until stiff peaks form. Fold in brown sugar. Spread over mixture in pan. Bake 35 minutes at 350°. Cool completely; cut into squares.

Caramel Cashew Bars

8 Rhodes Texas rolls,
  thawed and raised
1½ c chocolate chips
14 oz caramels, unwrapped
⅓ c evaporated milk

⅓ c butter
1⅔ c powdered sugar
2 c cashew halves
½ c semisweet chocolate chips

Press 4 rolls together and roll into a 9x13-inch rectangle. Place in a 9x13-inch pan sprayed with non-stick cooking spray. Sprinkle with 1½ cups chocolate chips. Repeat with remaining rolls and place over top of chocolate chips. Bake at 350° for 15 minutes. Let cool.

Place caramels, milk, and butter in medium saucepan. Melt on low heat, stirring occasionally until smooth. Remove from heat. Add powdered sugar and stir until smooth. Fold in cashews. Pour mixture over baked crust. Melt ½ cup chocolate chips in microwave, and drizzle over caramel layer. Refrigerate until firm.

Chocolate Cappuccino Brownies

BROWNIE LAYER:

4 oz fine-quality bittersweet chocolate
(not unsweetened), chopped
³/₄ stick (6 tbsp) unsalted butter,
cut into pieces
1 tbsp instant espresso powder,
dissolved in ¹/₂ tbsp
boiling water

³/₄ c sugar
1 tsp vanilla extract
2 large eggs
¹/₂ c all-purpose flour
¹/₄ tsp salt
¹/₂ c walnuts, chopped

CREAM CHEESE FROSTING:

4 oz cream cheese, softened
3 tbsp unsalted butter, softened
¾ c confectioners' sugar, sifted

½ tsp vanilla extract
½ tsp cinnamon

GLAZE:

3 oz fine-quality bittersweet chocolate (not unsweetened)
1 tbsp unsalted butter
¼ c heavy cream
2¼ tsp instant espresso powder, dissolved in ½ tbsp boiling water

Preheat oven to 350°, and butter and flour an 8-inch square baking pan, tapping out excess flour.

BROWNIE LAYER:

In a heavy 1½-quart saucepan, melt chocolate and butter with espresso mixture over low heat, stirring until smooth, and remove pan from heat. Cool mixture to lukewarm and whisk in sugar and vanilla. Add eggs, 1 at a time, whisking well until mixture is glossy and smooth. Stir in flour and salt until just combined and stir in walnuts.

Spread batter evenly in pan and bake in middle of oven 22–25 minutes, or until a tester comes out with crumbs adhering to it. Cool brownie layer completely in pan on a rack.

CREAM CHEESE FROSTING:

In a bowl with an electric mixer, beat cream cheese and butter until light and fluffy. Add confectioners' sugar, vanilla, and cinnamon, and beat until combined well. Spread frosting evenly over brownie layer. Chill brownies 1 hour, or until frosting is firm.

GLAZE:

In a double boiler or metal bowl set over a saucepan of barely simmering water, melt chocolate and butter with cream and espresso mixture, stirring until smooth, and remove top of double boiler or bowl from heat. Cool glaze to room temperature.

Spread glaze carefully over frosting. Chill brownies, covered, until cold, at least 3 hours.

Cut chilled brownies into 24 squares and remove them from pan while still cold. Serve brownies cold or at room temperature. Brownies keep, covered and chilled, in one layer, 5 days.

Cinnamon Toffee Bars

½ c butter
2 c brown sugar, packed
2 eggs, beaten
2 tsp vanilla extract
2 c all-purpose flour

2 tsp baking powder
¼ tsp salt
1 tsp ground cinnamon
1 c pecans, chopped
12 oz semisweet chocolate chips

Cook butter and brown sugar over low heat, in a saucepan, until mixture comes to a boil. Remove from heat and let cool.

Preheat oven to 350°. Grease a 12x18-inch jelly roll pan.

In a medium bowl, stir together butter mixture, eggs, and vanilla. Sift together flour, baking powder, salt, and cinnamon; stir into egg mixture until well blended. Then stir in pecans. Spread batter onto prepared jelly roll pan. Bake in preheated oven for 25 minutes. Remove from oven and immediately sprinkle chocolate chips over whole sheet. Let stand for 5 minutes, then spread chocolate evenly over entire surface. Cut into squares.

Candy Bar Squares

¾ c butter or margarine, softened
¼ c peanut butter
1 c brown sugar, packed
1 tsp baking soda
2 c quick oats
1½ c flour

1 egg
1 14-oz can sweetened
   condensed milk (not
   evaporated)
4 c candy bars, chopped (like
   Snickers or Milky Way)

Preheat oven to 350°. In large bowl, combine butter and peanut butter. Add brown sugar and baking soda; beat well. Stir in oats and flour. Reserve 1³/₄ cups crumb mixture.

Stir egg into remaining crumb mixture; press firmly on bottom of ungreased 15x10x1-inch baking pan. Bake 15 minutes.

Spread sweetened condensed milk over baked crust. Stir together remaining crumb mixture and candy bar pieces; sprinkle evenly over top. Bake 25 minutes or until golden. Cool. Cut into bars. Store covered at room temperature.

Butterscotch Bars

1 12-oz pkg butterscotch
    morsels
½ c butter or margarine
2 c graham cracker crumbs
1 c walnuts, finely chopped
1 8-oz pkg cream cheese,
    softened

1 14-oz can sweetened
    condensed milk (not
    evaporated)
1 egg
1 tsp vanilla extract

Preheat oven to 350°. Grease a 9x13-inch baking dish; set aside. In medium saucepan, melt morsels and butter over low heat, stirring often. Stir in crumbs and nuts. Press half of mixture into bottom of pan.

In large mixing bowl, with electric mixer on medium, beat cream cheese until fluffy. Beat in condensed milk, egg, and vanilla until smooth. Pour over crumb mixture in pan. Sprinkle remaining crumb mixture on top. Bake 25–30 minutes or until toothpick inserted in center comes out clean. Cool completely on wire rack. Refrigerate.

Coconut Bars

2 sticks margarine, melted
1 c sugar
1 egg, slightly beaten
½ c milk

1 c nuts, chopped
1 can coconut
1 c graham cracker crumbs
Whole graham crackers

Combine first 4 ingredients in a saucepan and bring to a boil; cook one minute, then add nuts, coconut, and cracker crumbs. Grease 9x13x2-inch pan. Line with whole graham crackers. Pour above mixture over whole graham crackers, then add another layer of whole graham crackers. Spread with icing.

ICING:

¾ stick margarine
2 c confectioners' sugar

1 tbsp vanilla extract
1 tbsp milk

Mix all ingredients together. Spread on top of graham crackers. Refrigerate for several hours to allow graham crackers to soften slightly. Cut into strips or squares.

Caramel Apple Bars

BASE:

2 c flour
2 c quick rolled oats
1½ c brown sugar, firmly packed

1 tsp baking soda
1¼ c butter, melted

FILLING:

½ c flour
20 oz (1½ c) caramel ice cream
   topping

2 c Golden Delicious apples,
   chopped and peeled
½ c walnuts, chopped

Heat oven to 350°. Grease 15x10x1-inch baking pan. In large bowl, mix base ingredients until crumbly. Press half of base mixture into bottom of greased pan. Bake 8–10 minutes. In a small pan, mix flour and caramel; bring to a boil over medium heat, 3–5 minutes or until mixture thickens, stirring constantly. Remove base from oven; sprinkle apples and walnuts over base. Pour caramel mixture over apples and walnuts. Sprinkle remaining base mix on and bake for 20–25 minutes or until golden brown. Cool; refrigerate for 30 minutes or until set. Cut into bars. Can also be served warm.

Speedy Brownies

2 c sugar
1¾ c flour
½ c baking cocoa
1 tsp salt

5 eggs
1 c vegetable oil
1 tsp vanilla extract
1 c semisweet chocolate chips

In a mixing bowl, combine first 7 ingredients; beat until smooth. Pour into a greased 9x13-inch baking pan. Sprinkle with chocolate chips. Bake at 350° for 30 minutes, or until a toothpick inserted near center comes out clean. Cool in pan on a wire rack.

Orange-Date Bars

1 c dates, chopped
⅓ c sugar
⅓ c vegetable oil
½ c orange juice
1 c flour

½ c pecans, chopped
1 egg
1½ tsp baking powder
1 tbsp orange peel, grated

Combine dates, sugar, oil, and juice in a saucepan. Cook 5 minutes to soften dates. Cool. Add remaining ingredients. Spread into a greased 8x8-inch pan. Bake at 350° for 25 minutes. Cool before cutting.

Peanut Butter Oatmeal Bars

½ c butter
½ c sugar
½ c brown sugar
1 egg

½ c peanut butter
½ tsp baking soda
¼ tsp salt

½ tsp vanilla extract
1 c flour
1 c oatmeal

TOPPING #1
1 c semisweet chocolate chips

TOPPING #2
½ c confectioners' sugar, sifted
¼ c peanut butter
2–4 tbsp cream or milk

Cream butter and sugars. Blend in egg, peanut butter, baking soda, salt, and vanilla. Stir in flour and oatmeal. Spread in 9x13-inch pan and bake at 350° for 20–25 minutes. (See toppings.) Remove from oven, and immediately sprinkle with chocolate chips. Let stand 5 minutes; spread over top. Combine confectioners' sugar, peanut butter, and milk; drizzle over chocolate layer. Cool; cut into bars.

White Chocolate Squares

1 12-oz pkg white chocolate
  chips, divided
¼ c butter or margarine
2 c flour
½ tsp baking powder
1 tsp vanilla extract

1 14-oz can sweetened
  condensed milk (not evaporated)
1 c pecans or walnuts,
  chopped
1 large egg
Confectioners' sugar

Preheat oven to 350°. Grease a 9x13-inch baking pan. In large saucepan over low heat, melt 1 cup chips and butter. Stir in flour and baking powder until blended. Stir in vanilla, sweetened condensed milk, nuts, egg, and remaining chips. Spoon mixture into prepared pan.

Bake 20–25 minutes. Cool. Sprinkle with confectioners' sugar; cut into squares. Store covered at room temperature.

Caramel Pecan Brownies

24 vanilla caramels
4 tbsp milk
4 eggs
1½ c sugar
½ stick butter, melted
1 tsp vanilla extract

1½ c flour
1 tsp baking powder
1 c pecans, chopped
1 tsp salt
Confectioners' sugar

Stir together caramels and milk over medium heat until caramels are melted. Set aside. In mixing bowl, beat eggs; gradually beat in sugar. Blend in butter, caramel mixture and vanilla. Stir together flour, baking powder, and salt; add to caramel mixture. Fold in pecans. Pour into greased baking pan. Bake at 350° for 30–40 minutes. Sift confectioners' sugar on top. Cut into bars.

Chewy Bars

1 box yellow cake mix
1 c light brown sugar, packed
2¾ c oil
4 eggs

1½ c milk
¼ c cinnamon
2 c nuts (optional)

Mix all dry ingredients. Blend eggs and milk together, beating slightly. Add to dry mix alternately with oil. Add nuts. Spread into an ungreased sheet pan. Bake at 350° for 20–25 minutes. Let cool for 30 minutes before cutting into squares.

Chocolate Peanut Bars

1 pkg (18¼ oz) white cake mix
1 c peanut butter, divided
1 egg
1 pkg (8 oz) cream cheese,
   softened

⅓ c milk
¼ c sugar
1 c (6 oz) semisweet
   chocolate chips
¾ c salted peanuts

In a mixing bowl, beat cake mix, ⅔ cup peanut butter, and egg until crumbly. Press into a greased 9x13-inch baking pan. In a mixing bowl, combine cream cheese and remaining peanut butter. Gradually beat in milk and sugar. Carefully spread over crust. Sprinkle with chocolate chips and peanuts.

Bake at 350° for 25–30 minutes or until edges are lightly browned and center is set. Cool completely before cutting. Store in refrigerator.

Caramel Brownies

2 c sugar
¾ c baking cocoa
1 c vegetable oil
4 eggs
¼ c milk
1½ c all-purpose flour
1 tsp salt

1 tsp baking powder
1 c (6 oz) semisweet chocolate
    chips
1 c chopped walnuts, divided
1 pkg (14 oz) caramels
1 can (14 oz) sweetened
    condensed milk (not
    evaporated)

In a mixing bowl, combine sugar, cocoa, oil, eggs, and milk. In a different bowl, combine flour, salt, and baking powder; add to egg mixture and mix until combined. Fold in chocolate chips and ½ cup walnuts. Spoon two-thirds of batter into a greased 9x13-inch baking pan. Bake at 350° for 12 minutes.

Meanwhile, in a saucepan, heat caramels and sweetened condensed milk over low heat until caramels are melted. Pour over baked brownie layer. Sprinkle with remaining walnuts. Drop remaining batter by teaspoonfuls over caramel layer; carefully swirl brownie batter with a knife. Bake 35–40 minutes longer or until toothpick inserted near center comes out with moist crumbs. Cool.

Seven-Layer Bars

½ c butter
1 c graham cracker crumbs
1 c flaked coconut
6 oz butterscotch chips

6 oz chocolate chips
1 c nuts, chopped
1 can sweetened condensed
    milk (not evaporated)

Preheat oven to 325°. Melt butter in a 9x13-inch pan. Add next 5 ingredients in layers and carefully pour sweetened condensed milk on top. Bake for 25–30 minutes or until slightly brown.

Blueberry Cheese Squares

1 roll prepared cookie dough
    (lemon, butterscotch, or
    other flavor)
1 8-oz pkg cream cheese, softened
1 c sour cream

¼ c sugar
1 egg
½ tsp vanilla extract
1 can blueberry pie filling

Preheat oven to 375°. Slice dough in ¼-inch slices. Overlap in ungreased 9x13-inch pan. Bake for 12–15 minutes, then allow to cool a few minutes. Meanwhile, combine cream cheese, sour cream, sugar, egg, and vanilla. Beat until smooth. Pour pie filling over cookie crust. Top with cream mixture and bake for 25–30 minutes. Serves 12.

Chocolate Syrup Brownies

½ c butter or margarine, softened
1 c sugar
1 16-oz can (1½ c) chocolate
   flavored syrup

4 eggs
1¼ c flour
1 c walnuts, chopped
Quick frosting (see next page)

Cream butter and sugar; beat in eggs. Blend in syrup and flour; stir in nuts. Pour into greased 9x13-inch pan. Bake at 350° for 30–35 minutes. Cool slightly; top with Quick Frosting.

Quick Frosting:

⅔ c sugar	3 tbsp butter
3 tbsp milk	½ c chocolate chips

In a saucepan, mix first 3 ingredients, then bring to a boil; boil for 30 seconds. Remove from heat; stir in chocolate chips until melted. Will be thin. Spread over brownies. Cool; cut into bars.

Rhubarb Bars

3 c cut rhubarb
1½ c sugar
1 tsp vanilla extract
2 tbsp cornstarch
¼ c water
1½ c oatmeal

1 c brown sugar
1 c shortening (part margarine)
½ c walnuts, chopped
1½ c flour
½ tsp baking soda

Cook first 5 ingredients until thick. In a separate bowl, mix remaining ingredients; pat ¾ mixture into a 9x13-inch pan. Pour and spread cooked rhubarb mixture over crust. Sprinkle remaining crumbs on top. Bake at 375° for 30–35 minutes.

Chocolate Caramel Bars

2 c flour
1 c brown sugar
½ c butter
1 c pecans, finely chopped

⅔ c butter
½ c brown sugar
1 c butterscotch chips
1 c semisweet chocolate chips

Mix flour, 1 cup brown sugar, ½ cup butter in a food processor or with a pastry blender. Pat this crust into bottom of a 9x13-inch pan. Sprinkle pecans on top of crust. Melt ⅔ cup butter and ½ cup brown sugar and cook until bubbly (about 2–3 minutes), then pour mixture over top of crust. Bake at 350° for 15–20 minutes, until melted butter and sugar are bubbling on top and crust is lightly browned. Remove from oven and sprinkle a mixture of butterscotch chips and semisweet chocolate chips over top. Let chips melt and then swirl them together over top of crust. Cut while still warm into 48 squares.

Frosted Peanut Butter Bars

½ c peanut butter
⅓ c shortening
1½ c brown sugar, packed
2 eggs
1 tsp vanilla extract

1½ c all-purpose flour
1½ tsp baking powder
½ tsp salt
¼ c milk

FROSTING:

⅔ c creamy peanut butter
½ c shortening

4 c confectioners' sugar
⅓ to ½ c milk

TOPPING:

½ c semisweet chocolate chips   1 tsp shortening

In a mixing bowl, cream peanut butter, shortening, and brown sugar. Beat in eggs and vanilla. Combine flour, baking powder, and salt; gradually add to creamed mixture. Add milk; mix well. Transfer to a greased 15x10x1-inch baking pan. Bake at 350° for 16–20 minutes or until a toothpick inserted near center comes out clean. Cool.

For frosting, in a mixing bowl, cream peanut butter, shortening, and confectioners' sugar. Gradually beat in enough milk to achieve spreading consistency. Frost bars. Melt chocolate chips and shortening; stir until smooth. Drizzle over frosting. Refrigerate.

Cakes

But if we have food and clothing,
we will be content with that.

1 Timothy 6:8

Almond Lemon Cake

8 egg whites
1 dash cream of tartar
1 c sugar, divided
2 c flour
1 tsp baking powder
$\frac{1}{8}$ tsp salt
1 c butter or margarine, softened

1½ tbsp lemon peel, grated
1 tbsp lemon juice
1 c sour cream extract
2 tsp vanilla extract
1 c blanched almonds,
   finely chopped

In a bowl, beat egg whites with cream of tartar until stiff. Gradually beat in ½ cup sugar. In another bowl, stir together flour, baking powder, and salt.

In a large bowl, cream butter or margarine with remaining ½ cup sugar. Beat in lemon peel, lemon juice, sour cream, and vanilla. Stir flour mixture into butter mixture, along with about ⅓ of beaten egg whites. Fold in rest of egg whites gently but thoroughly. Stir in almonds. Turn batter into greased and floured tube pan. Bake at 350° for about 70 minutes, or until it tests done with a toothpick. Cool on a wire rack.

Almond Pound Cake

1 c butter, softened
2 c white sugar
6 eggs, room temperature
1¾ c all-purpose flour
½ tsp salt
2 tsp almond extract

8 oz almond paste
1 c confectioners' sugar
4 tbsp milk
½ c blanched almonds
4 drops red food coloring
4 drops green food coloring

Preheat oven to 325°. Grease and flour a 10-inch Bundt pan. In a large bowl, cream butter and sugar together until well mixed with an electric mixer. Add eggs, one at a time, and beat until mixture is light and fluffy. Blend in flour and salt. Mix in almond extract. Turn batter into prepared pan. Bake for 60 minutes, or until a toothpick inserted in center of cake comes out clean. Cool in pan for 10 minutes. Remove from pan, and transfer to a wire rack to continue cooling.

Break off tablespoon-sized pieces of almond paste, and shape into holly leaves. Using the tip of a knife, score shaped holly leaves to resemble veins in leaves. Mix green food coloring with a small amount of water and brush holly leaves, repeating until desired color is reached. Set aside on waxed paper. Break off 2 tablespoons of almond paste, and knead in several drops of red food coloring. When color of almond paste is a bright red, break off smaller pieces. Roll into balls to resemble holly berries. Place on waxed paper. In a small bowl, combine 1 cup confectioners' sugar and milk. Mix until smooth. When cake has cooled, drizzle with confectioners' sugar glaze. Top with blanched almonds, and garnish with marzipan holly leaves and berries.

Chocolate Caramel Cake

1²⁄₃ c flour	½ c shortening
1½ c sugar	2 eggs
²⁄₃ c cocoa powder	1½ tsp vanilla extract
1½ tsp baking powder	30 caramels
1 tsp salt	1 can sweetened condensed milk
1½ c buttermilk	(not evaporated)

Beat first 9 ingredients in large mixing bowl on low speed, scraping sides of bowl, until blended. Beat on high, scraping sides occasionally for an additional 3 minutes. Pour half the mixture into a greased and floured 9x13-inch pan, and bake at 350° for 15 minutes. In the meantime, melt caramels and sweetened condensed milk together. Spread over warm cake. Put remaining cake mixture on top of caramel mixture. Bake an additional 15 minutes, or until done. May be served warm with vanilla ice cream for a tasty treat.

Snicker Doodle Cake

1 German chocolate cake mix	⅓ c milk
1 14-oz pkg caramels	¾ c chocolate chips
1 stick margarine	1 c walnuts, chopped

Prepare cake mix, following package directions. Pour half the batter into a greased 9x13-inch greased pan. Bake at 350° for 20 minutes. Melt caramels with margarine and milk in saucepan over low heat, stirring frequently. Pour over baked cake. Sprinkle with chocolate chips and nuts. Spoon remaining cake batter over caramel layer. Bake at 250° for 20 minutes. Increase temperature to 350° and bake an additional 10 minutes.

Angel Cake Surprise

1 10-inch tube pan angel food
  cake or pound cake
1 3-oz pkg strawberry-
  flavored gelatin
1 15-oz can sliced peaches
3 bananas

1 20-oz can crushed
  pineapple, drained (optional)
1 5-oz pkg instant
  vanilla pudding mix
1 8-oz container frozen
  whipped topping, thawed

Break angel food or pound cake into bite-size pieces. Put into a 9x13-inch pan (preferably glass). Dissolve 1 package of flavored gelatin in 1 cup of hot water and pour over cake pieces, spreading to the edges of pan. Drain peaches and pour juice over gelatin in pan. Slice bananas on top of gelatin. Arrange peach slices on top of banana slices. If desired, add crushed pineapple. Prepare instant pudding according to instructions on box and spread evenly over fruit. Spread whipped topping on top of pudding. Try to keep layers separate. Refrigerate at least 2 hours before serving.

Apple Bundt Cake

2 c apples: peeled, cored,
  and diced
1 tbsp sugar
1 tsp ground cinnamon
3 c flour
3 tsp baking powder
½ tsp salt

2 c sugar
1 c vegetable oil
¼ c orange juice
2½ tsp vanilla extract
4 eggs
1 c walnuts, chopped
¼ c confectioners' sugar

Preheat oven to 350°. Grease and flour a 10-inch Bundt or tube pan. In a medium bowl, combine diced apples, 1 tablespoon sugar, and 1 tsp cinnamon; set aside. Sift together flour, baking powder, and salt; set aside. In a large bowl, combine 2 cups sugar, oil, orange juice, vanilla, and eggs. Beat at high speed until smooth. Stir in flour mixture. Fold in chopped walnuts. Pour ⅓ of the batter into prepared pan. Sprinkle with ½ of the apple mixture. Alternate layers of batter and filling, ending with batter. Bake for 55–60 minutes, or until top springs back when lightly touched. Let cool in pan for 10 minutes, then turn out onto a wire rack and cool completely. Sprinkle with confectioners' sugar.

Apple Sheet Cake

PASTRY:

3 c flour
1½ tsp baking powder
1 tsp salt

½ c shortening
1 c cold milk

APPLE FILLING:

3 lbs apples: peeled,
  cored, and sliced
1 c sugar

1 tsp ground cinnamon
2 tbsp flour
½ c butter

FROSTING:

2½ c confectioners' sugar
3 tbsp milk

⅓ c butter, softened
½ tsp vanilla extract

Preheat oven to 400°. In a large bowl, combine 3 cups flour, baking powder, and salt. Cut in shortening to consistency of coarse crumbs. Stir in milk slowly until completely blended. Separate dough into two balls. Roll out one ball of dough to fit a 15x10-inch pan with some dough extending over edge of pan.

In a large bowl, combine sliced apples, sugar, cinnamon, and 2 tablespoons flour. Place filling in an even layer over prepared crust. Thinly slice ½ cup butter and evenly distribute over apples. Roll out remaining dough and place over apple filling. Seal edges and prick top all over with a fork. Bake in preheated oven for 30 minutes. Cool 5 minutes before frosting.

To Make Frosting:
In a small bowl, combine ingredients; beat until smooth and creamy.

Butter Cookie Almond Wreath Cake

1 c unsalted butter, room
    temperature
1 c almond paste, room
    temperature

1 c confectioners' sugar
1 tsp almond extract
2 egg yolks
½ tsp salt
2½ c flour

In a large mixing bowl, cream together butter, almond paste, and sugar until very smooth. Blend in almond extract and egg yolks. In a separate bowl, stir together salt and flour, then blend into butter mixture. Chill dough for 30 minutes. Preheat oven to 350°. Cover several cookie sheets with parchment paper. Cut off portions of dough and shape into ropes about the thickness of your thumb, each 1 inch longer than the previous, beginning at 4 inches and ending at 18 inches. You will have 15 strands. Shape each strand into a circle and place on parchment-covered baking sheets. Bake for 10 minutes or until pale gold. Cool.

ROYAL ICING:

1 lb (3–4 c) confectioners' sugar   1 tsp almond extract
1–2 egg whites

Place powdered sugar in large bowl. Add one egg white and almond extract. Mix with electric beater until smooth and well blended. If necessary, add part or all of the second egg white. The icing needs to be thin enough to press through the fine tip of a pastry bag. (In place of a pastry bag, you can use a cone made from waxed paper. Snip off bottom of cone to form a fine-tip opening.) Spoon icing into pastry bag (or waxed paper cone).

TO ASSEMBLE CAKE:
Place largest cookie ring on a serving plate. Press Royal Icing through pastry bag in a zigzag pattern all the way around the ring. Top with next largest ring. Repeat zigzag piping procedure. Continue stacking and frosting rings to form a balanced tower. Decorate the top with a fresh rose and the sides with flags, flowers, marzipan candies, or cracker bonbons, using Royal Icing to adhere them to the cake. To serve cake, lift top part of the tower off, and break remaining rings into 2- or 3-inch pieces.

Snowball Cake

2 envelopes unflavored gelatin	1 8-oz can crushed pineapple, drained
4 tbsp cold water	2 large containers Cool Whip
1 c boiling water	1 angel food cake
1 c sugar	1 small can coconut
2 tbsp lemon juice	

Mix gelatin with cold water. Add boiling water, sugar, lemon juice, and pineapple. Set in refrigerator to thicken for 30 minutes. Fold in 1 container of Cool Whip. Set aside. Crumble half of cake in 9x13-inch pan (bite-size pieces). Spoon half of mixture over cake. Repeat with other half. Frost with 1 container of Cool Whip. Sprinkle with coconut.

Black Forest Cake

2 20-oz cans tart pitted cherries, undrained
1 c sugar
¼ c cornstarch
1½ tsp vanilla extract

2 9-inch chocolate cake layers, baked and cooled
3 c cold whipping cream
⅓ c confectioners' sugar

Drain cherries, reserving ½ cup juice. Combine reserved cherry juices, cherries, sugar, and cornstarch in saucepan. Cook and stir over low heat until thickened. Add vanilla; stir. Divide each cake layer in half horizontally. Crumble one half layer; set aside. Beat cold whipping cream and confectioners' sugar in a large bowl with an electric mixer on high until stiff peaks form. Reserve 1½ cups whipped cream for decorative piping.

Place one cake layer on a serving plate. Spread with 1 cup whipped cream; top with ¾ cup cherry topping. Top with second cake layer, 1 cup whipped cream, and ¾ cup cherry topping; top with third cake layer. Frost cake sides with remaining whipped cream; pat gently with reserved cake crumbs.

Spoon reserved 1½ cups whipped cream into pastry bag fitted with star tip; pipe around top and bottom edges of cake. Spoon remaining topping over top of cake.

Red Velvet Cake

½ c shortening
1½ c sugar
2 eggs
2 tbsp cocoa
1½ oz red food coloring
1 tsp salt

2½ c flour
1 tsp vanilla extract
1 c buttermilk
1 tsp baking soda
1 tbsp vinegar

Cream shortening; add sugar gradually. Add eggs, one at a time; beat well.
Make paste of cocoa and coloring; add to creamed mixture. Add salt, flour,

and vanilla alternately with buttermilk, beating well after each addition. Sprinkle soda over vinegar; pour vinegar over batter. Stir until thoroughly mixed. Bake in 3 8-inch square pans or 2 9-inch square pans for 30 minutes at 350°.

CREAM CHEESE FROSTING:

2 3-oz pkgs cream cheese, softened	1 tsp vanilla extract
6 tbsp butter, softened	2 c confectioners' sugar, sifted

Blend all ingredients until smooth.

Molasses Cake

1 tsp baking powder	2 c flour
1 tsp soda	1 c molasses
1 tsp cinnamon	1 egg
1 tsp nutmeg	½ c butter
¾ c sugar	1 c sour cream

Mix all dry ingredients together. Add molasses, egg, butter, and sour cream together. Mix well. Bake at 350° for 30–35 minutes. Bakes a 9x13-inch, 2-layer cake.

Candy

"Do not work for food that spoils,
but for food that endures to eternal life,
which the Son of Man will give you.
On him God the Father has placed his seal of approval."

JOHN 6:27

Soft Peanut Butter Peanut Brittle
A softer alternative to a traditional holiday favorite

2 c sugar
¼ c water
1½ c light corn syrup
2 c salted peanuts

2–2½ c peanut butter
½ tsp vanilla extract
1½ tsp baking soda

Combine sugar and water in heavy saucepan. Bring mixture to full rolling boil over high heat, stirring constantly. Stir in corn syrup. Cook to hard-crack stage, 300°. Meanwhile, mix peanuts, peanut butter, and vanilla. Remove syrup from heat; at once add peanut butter mixture and baking soda; stir. Working quickly, pour onto buttered cookie sheet; spread with fork. Cool; break into pieces.

Fantastic Fudge

⅔ c evaporated milk
1⅔ c sugar
1½ c chocolate chips

1½ c miniature marshmallows
½ tsp salt
1 tsp vanilla extract

Combine milk and sugar; bring to a boil for 5 minutes. Add chocolate chips and marshmallows. Stir until blended. Add salt and vanilla and pour into a buttered 8-inch square baking dish to cool.

Flavor variations for this recipe are on the following page.

MOCHA: Dissolve 2 teaspoons instant coffee granules in 1 teaspoon hot water. Add with chocolate.

MINT: Add ¾ mint chips, ¾ chocolate chips.

MARBLE: Make fudge with white chocolate and drizzle in melted chocolate chips.

CHOCOLATE ORANGE: Add 2 teaspoons freshly grated orange peel.

PEANUT BUTTER: Substitute peanut butter chips for chocolate chips.

WHITE ALMOND: Substitute white chocolate chips and ½ cup slivered almonds.

MAPLE: Substitute butterscotch chips, and add maple flavoring to taste.

Sticks and Stones Candy Bark

1 11-oz pkg butterscotch morsels,
  divided
1½ c semisweet chocolate morsels
½ c creamy peanut butter

2 c dry-roasted peanuts
1 10-oz pkg semisweet
  chocolate-covered raisins
2 c thin pretzel sticks

Butter a 9x13-inch glass baking dish. Microwave 1⅓ cup butterscotch morsels, semisweet morsels, and peanut butter in large, microwave-safe bowl on high for 1 minute; stir. Microwave at additional 10- to 20-second intervals, stirring until smooth. Add pretzels, peanuts, and chocolate-covered raisins; stir well to coat. Spread into prepared baking dish. Place remaining butterscotch morsels in small, heavy-duty plastic bag. Microwave on medium-high (70 percent) power for 30 seconds; knead bag to mix. Microwave at additional 10- to 20-second intervals, kneading until smooth. Cut tiny corner from bag; squeeze to drizzle over candy. Refrigerate for 1 hour or until firm. Break into bite-size pieces.

Festive Holiday Bark

16 oz vanilla-flavored
  confectioners' coating
2 c small pretzel twists

$\frac{1}{2}$ c red and green
  candy-coated chocolate

Line a cookie sheet with waxed paper or parchment paper. Place confectioners' coating in a microwave-safe bowl. Microwave for 2½ minutes. Stir; microwave at 30-second intervals until completely melted and smooth. Place pretzels and candy-coated chocolate pieces in a large bowl. Pour melted coating over and stir until well coated. Spread onto waxed paper-lined baking sheet. Let stand until firm or place in refrigerator to set up faster. Store in a container at room temperature.

Milk Chocolate Popcorn

12 c popcorn, popped
2½ c salted peanuts
1 c light corn syrup

1 11½-oz pkg milk chocolate
  morsels
¼ c butter or margarine

Preheat oven to 300°. Grease a large roasting pan. Line a large bowl or serving plate with waxed paper. Combine popcorn and nuts in prepared roasting pan. Combine corn syrup, morsels, and butter in medium, heavy-duty saucepan. Cook over medium heat, stirring constantly, until mixture boils. Pour over popcorn; toss well to coat. Bake, stirring frequently, for 30–40 minutes. Cool slightly in pan; remove to prepared serving plate. Store in airtight container for up to two weeks.

Candied Apples

1²/₃ c cinnamon red hot candies
12 craft sticks

2 tbsp water
12 apples

Insert craft sticks into apples. Line a baking sheet with waxed paper. Pour candies and water in a heavy-bottomed saucepan over medium-high heat. Occasionally brushing down sides of pan with a heat-resistant pastry brush, heat candy to 300–310°, or until a small amount of syrup dropped into cold water forms hard, brittle threads. Remove from heat and let cool slightly. Dip apples into hot liquid and place on waxed paper to harden.

Clothesline Candy

3 c sugar
½ c corn syrup
2 tbsp butter

1 c dates
1 c nuts
1 tsp vanilla extract

Mix first 3 ingredients and cook to medium-ball stage (244–248°). Remove from heat. Add dates and nuts. Boil 3 minutes. Remove from heat and let sit until almost cool. Add vanilla. Beat like fudge. Have dishtowel soaking in ice water. Pour candy onto wrung-out wet towel. Roll back and forth into roll. Roll up in towel. Tie each end with a string. Hang from clothesline to harden overnight. Take out of towel and slice.

Chocolate Orange Truffles

¼ c unsalted butter
3 tbsp heavy whipping cream
4 1-oz squares semisweet
    chocolate, chopped
2 tbsp orange juice

1 tsp orange peel, grated
4 1-oz squares semisweet
    chocolate, chopped
1 tbsp vegetable oil

In a medium saucepan, bring butter and cream to a boil over medium-high heat. Remove from heat. Add 4 squares chocolate, orange juice, and orange peel; stir until melted and smooth. Pour truffle mixture into a shallow bowl or a 9x5-inch loaf pan. Chill until firm, about 2 hours. Line 2 baking sheets with waxed paper. Shape chilled truffle mixture by rounded teaspoons into small balls. Place on prepared baking sheets. Chill until firm, about 30 minutes.

In top of a double boiler set over simmering (not boiling) water, heat remaining chocolate and oil, stirring until melted and smooth. Transfer chocolate mixture to a bowl. Cool completely. Drop truffles into melted chocolate mixture. Using 2 forks, lift out truffles, tapping gently on side of bowl to allow excess coating to drip back in bowl. Return truffles to baking sheets lined with waxed paper, and chill until set.

Microwave Dump Fudge

1 lb confectioners' sugar, sifted
1 stick real butter, sliced
½ c cocoa

¼ c milk
1½ tsp vanilla extract
½ c nuts, chopped (if desired)

Dump confectioners' sugar, butter slices, cocoa, and milk into microwave-safe bowl. Microwave on high for 2 minutes. Remove; stir vigorously to blend. Add vanilla and nuts. Pour into an 8-inch square pan lined with foil and buttered. Refrigerate until firm.

Chocolate Brittle Surprise

35 unsalted soda crackers
1 c butter
1 c brown sugar, packed

2 c semisweet chocolate chips
1 c pecans, chopped (optional)

Preheat oven to 350°. Cover cookie sheet with foil. Spray foil with cooking oil spray. Place crackers on foil in 5x7-inch rows. Microwave butter on high for 2 minutes. Add brown sugar and stir. Microwave on high for 2 more minutes, stirring every 30 seconds.

Pour over crackers. Bake 17 to 20 minutes (should bubble but not burn). Sprinkle chocolate chips over hot crackers. Spread after 2 minutes (chips have softened). Sprinkle nuts on top. Refrigerate 1 hour. Break into pieces. Can be frozen.

Peanut Butter Cups

2–3 lb melting chocolate
1 c graham cracker crumbs
   (7½ whole crackers)

2 sticks butter, melted
¾ c peanut butter
1 lb box confectioners' sugar

Coat small paper cup liners with melted chocolate to cup edge. Chill. Mix remaining ingredients; add mixture and cover with chocolate. Chill until firm.

Christmas Crunch

2 c sugar
⅔ c light corn syrup
½ c water
3 tbsp butter

1 tsp vanilla extract
½ tsp baking soda
2 c crispy rice cereal
1 c cashews

Grease one 10x15-inch baking pan. In a large saucepan over medium heat, combine sugar, corn syrup, and water; bring to a boil, stirring constantly until sugar is dissolved. Continue to cook, without stirring, until candy thermometer reads 300°. Remove from heat; stir in butter, vanilla, and baking soda. Add cereal and cashews; pour into prepared pan and allow to cool. Break into pieces and store in airtight container.

Cracker Candy

½ lb butter
¾ c sugar
¼ of a 16-oz pkg saltine crackers

2 c semisweet chocolate chips
¾ c walnuts, chopped

Preheat oven to 425°. Melt butter in a saucepan over medium heat. Add sugar and stir occasionally until mixture comes to boil. Boil for 3 minutes and stir to keep from burning. Place crackers on a cookie sheet and drizzle with sugar mixture. Bake for 5 minutes or until edges begin to brown. Remove from oven and sprinkle chocolate chips on top, spreading them out as they melt. Sprinkle nuts on top and gently press into chocolate. Allow to cool and break into pieces. Refrigerate until ready to serve.

Hard Rock Candy

3³/₄ c sugar
1¹/₂ c light corn syrup
1 c water

2 tsp cinnamon oil
1 tsp red food coloring
Confectioners' sugar

Roll edges of two 16-inch square pieces of heavy-duty aluminum foil. Sprinkle foil very generously with confectioners' sugar. In a large heavy saucepan combine sugar, corn syrup, and water. Heat over medium-high heat, stirring constantly until sugar dissolves. Stop stirring and heat until a candy thermometer reads 300°–310°. Remove from heat and stir in cinnamon oil and food coloring. Pour over prepared foil; let cool and harden. Crack into pieces and store in an airtight container.

Basic Butter Cream Fondant
The following fondant recipe is used as the filling for chocolate-covered candy

2 sticks butter (room temperature)

2 lb confectioners' sugar
7 oz marshmallow cream

Mix all ingredients together with your hands, kneading until smooth. Makes about 2½ pounds of fondant.

Coat candy molds with chocolate flavor of choice, place small amount of fondant on chilled chocolate. Coat with chocolate to seal, and chill.

Variations:

CHOCOLATE CREAM:
⅓ recipe Butter Cream Fondant ¼ c cocoa

PEANUT BUTTER CREAM:
⅓ recipe Butter Cream Fondant ¼ c creamy peanut butter

PEPPERMINT:
⅓ recipe Butter Cream Fondant Peppermint flavoring to taste

MAPLE-NUT CREAM:

$\frac{1}{3}$ recipe Butter Cream Fondant
Maple flavoring to taste

$\frac{1}{2}$ c walnuts or pecans,
    finely chopped

CHERRY-NUT CREAM:

$\frac{1}{3}$ recipe Butter Cream Fondant
$\frac{1}{4}$ c maraschino cherry pieces

Cherry juice
$\frac{1}{4}$ c walnuts, chopped

Mix cut-up pieces of maraschino cherries, cherry juice for flavoring, and cut-up walnuts. If recipe is too runny, add more confectioners' sugar.

Melt In Your Mouth Toffee

1 lb butter or margarine
1 c sugar
1 c brown sugar, packed

1 c walnuts, chopped
2 c semisweet chocolate chips

In a heavy saucepan, combine butter and sugars. Cook over medium heat, stirring constantly until mixture boils. Boil to brittle stage, 300°, without stirring. Remove from heat. Pour nuts and chocolate chips into a 9x13-inch dish. Pour hot mixture over nuts and chocolate. Let mixture cool and break into pieces before serving.

Microwave Peanut Brittle

1 c raw peanuts
1 c sugar
½ c light corn syrup
⅛ tsp salt

1 tsp butter
1 tsp vanilla extract
½ tsp baking soda

Mix peanuts, sugar, syrup, and salt in a 1½-quart glass casserole dish. Microwave on high for 8 minutes, stirring after 4 minutes. Stir in butter and vanilla, then cook for 2 more minutes. Stir in baking soda. Pour onto a greased baking sheet. Using two forks, stretch until thin. Cool, then break into pieces.

Christmas Turtle Candies

4 oz pecan halves
24 caramels

1 c semisweet chocolate chips
1 tsp shortening

Preheat oven to 300°. Cover cookie sheet with aluminum foil, shiny side up. Lightly grease foil with vegetable oil spray. Place 3 pecan halves in a Y shape on foil. Place 1 caramel candy in center of each Y. Repeat. Bake just until caramel is melted, about 9 to 10 minutes. Heat shortening and chocolate chips over low heat just until chocolate is melted. Spread over candies and refrigerate for 30 minutes.

Christmas Lollipops

1 lb white chocolate, broken into
   small pieces
1/4 c walnuts, finely chopped
1 tsp unsalted butter

36 candy stick molds
36 swizzle sticks (or candy
   sticks)

Combine chocolate and nuts in a stainless-steel bowl over a pan of simmering water. Stir mixture with a wooden spoon until chocolate melts and is creamy and smooth. Add butter and stir to melt. Spoon about 1 tablespoon of mixture into molds fitted with sticks. Smooth out top of each candy with a thin knife. Chill until candy sets, 2 to 3 hours. Remove candy from molds and store in layers of parchment or waxed paper in an airtight container. Will keep for up to 2 weeks.

Rocky Road Squares

3 lb milk chocolate   10 oz miniature marshmallows
½ lb butter, softened   3 lb peanuts

Melt chocolate; stir until smooth. Add butter and mix well (will be thick but warm). Set in cold place until it thickens around edges. Stir occasionally while cooling. Bring into warm room and stir 5 to 10 minutes until creamy and thinner. Add marshmallows and peanuts. Pour on waxed paper-lined cookie sheet; press ¾ inch thick. Cool. Cut in squares at room temperature.

No-Fuss Caramel Corn
(for microwave)

3 qt popcorn, popped
1 c brown sugar, packed
½ c butter or margarine

¼ c light corn syrup
¼ tsp salt
½ tsp baking soda

Place popcorn in large brown paper bag; set aside. Combine sugar, butter, corn syrup, and salt in 2-quart glass bowl. Microwave on high 3–4 minutes, stirring after each minute. Microwave 2 more minutes. Stir in baking soda. Pour over popcorn in bag. Close bag and shake well. Microwave 1 minute and shake again. Microwave on high 1 minute more, shake well, and pour onto 2 cookie sheets. Cool and stir to separate popcorn.

White Chocolate Covered Pretzels

6 1-oz squares white chocolate   ¼ c red and green candy sprinkles
1 15-oz pkg mini twist pretzels

Melt white chocolate in top of a double boiler, stirring constantly. Dip pretzel halfway into white chocolate, completely covering half of the pretzel. Roll in sprinkles if desired, and lay on waxed paper. Continue process until all of the white chocolate is finished. Place in refrigerator for 15 minutes to harden. Store in airtight container.

Peanut Butter Fudge

2 c sugar
½ c milk

1½ c peanut butter
1 jar (7 oz) marshmallow cream

In a saucepan, bring sugar and milk to a boil. Boil for 3 minutes. Add peanut butter and marshmallow cream; mix well and fast. Quickly pour into a buttered pan. Size of pan is according to how thick you like your fudge. Chill until set. Cut into squares.

Peanut Patties

2½ c sugar
1 c milk
⅔ c light corn syrup

Pinch of salt
4 c raw peanuts

Boil to soft-ball stage. Add:

4 tbsp butter
½ tsp vanilla extract

1½ c confectioners' sugar
Red food coloring

Mix well. Drop by teaspoonfuls onto waxed paper.

Cookies

*"Therefore I tell you, do not worry about your life,
what you will eat or drink;
or about your body, what you will wear.
Is not life more important than food,
and the body more important than clothes?"*

MATTHEW 6:25

Snowflakes

1 c butter-flavored shortening	1 tsp vanilla extract
1 3-oz pkg cream cheese, softened	1 tsp orange peel
1 c sugar	2½ c flour
1 egg yolk	½ tsp salt
	¼ tsp ground cinnamon

Preheat oven to 350°. In a medium bowl, cream together shortening, cream cheese, and sugar. Beat in egg yolk, vanilla, and orange peel. Continue creaming until light and fluffy. Gradually stir in flour, salt, and cinnamon. Fill cookie press, and form cookies on ungreased cookie sheet. Bake in pre-heated oven for 10 to 12 minutes. Remove from cookie sheet, and cool on wire racks.

Christmas Chinese Chews

¾ c flour, sifted
1 c nuts, chopped
1 tsp baking powder
2 eggs

1 c sugar
1 pinch salt
1 pkg dates, chopped
1 tsp vanilla extract

Mix ingredients and bake in a 9x3-inch ungreased pan at 375° for 20 minutes. While hot, cut into ½-inch strips, ½ inch wide, and roll in granulated sugar.

Christmas Stars

¾ c butter, softened
1 c sugar
2 eggs
1 tsp vanilla extract
2½ c flour

1 tsp baking powder
¼ tsp salt
¼ c green decorator sugar
  (optional)
6 tbsp strawberry jam

In a large bowl, cream butter and sugar until light and fluffy. Gradually add eggs and vanilla. Mix well. Sift together flour, baking powder, and salt. Stir flour mixture into butter mixture until well blended. Refrigerate dough for 3 hours. Preheat oven to 350°. Grease several cookie sheets.

On a floured surface, roll out ½ of the dough at a time to ⅛-inch thickness. Cut dough into star shapes using a 3- to 4-inch star cookie cutter. Using a 1- to 2-inch star cookie cutter, cut a star into the center of half of the big stars. If desired, sprinkle colored sugar on cookies with center cut out. Put onto prepared cookie sheets about 1 inch apart, and bake for 6 to 8 minutes. After cookies cool completely, spread 1 teaspoon of jam in center of each cookie that does not have a star cut out in the middle. Place a cookie with a cutout on top of the layer of jam. Pack cookies in a covered tin to preserve freshness.

Christmas Spice Cookies

¾ c sugar
⅔ c butter or margarine,
  softened
¼ c orange juice
½ c dark corn syrup
½ c dark molasses
4½ c flour

¾ c whole wheat flour
2 tsp ground ginger
1 tsp baking soda
1 tsp salt
½ tsp ground cloves
½ tsp ground nutmeg
½ tsp ground allspice

In a mixing bowl, cream sugar and butter. Blend in orange juice, corn syrup, and molasses. In a separate bowl, combine flours, ginger, baking soda, salt, cloves, nutmeg, and allspice. Add to creamed mixture; mix well. Chill 3 to 4 hours or overnight. Roll a portion of dough on a lightly floured surface to ¼-inch thickness. Cut into desired shapes. Place 2 inches apart on greased baking sheets. Repeat with remaining dough. Bake at 350° for 12 to 14 minutes. Cookies will be soft and chewy if baked 12 minutes, crunchy if baked longer.

Mexican Chocolate Sticks

1 c butter, softened	1 tsp cinnamon
1½ c confectioners' sugar	2 envelopes (1 oz each)
1 egg	premelted chocolate
1 tsp vanilla extract	2½ c flour

Mix butter and sugar. Add egg, vanilla, cinnamon, and chocolate. Blend in flour. With star plate in cookie press, form 4-inch fingers on an ungreased baking sheet. Bake at 375° for 5 minutes, or until set. Cool.

Chocolate Glaze:

1 c confectioners' sugar
1 envelope premelted chocolate

2 tbsp (or more) milk
Colored sprinkles

Blend first 3 ingredients; drizzle over cookies. Top with colored sprinkles.

Chocolate Snowballs

1¼ c butter
⅔ c sugar
1 tsp vanilla extract
2 c flour

⅛ tsp salt
½ c cocoa powder, unsweetened
2 c pecans, chopped
½ c confectioners' sugar

In a medium bowl, cream butter and sugar until light and fluffy. Stir in vanilla. Sift together flour, salt, and cocoa; stir into creamed mixture. Mix in pecans until well blended. Cover, and chill for at least 2 hours.

Preheat oven to 350°. Roll chilled dough into 1-inch balls. Place on ungreased cookie sheets about 2 inches apart. Bake for 20 minutes in preheated oven. Roll in confectioners' sugar when cooled.

Pecan Tassies

½ c butter   1 c flour
1 3-oz pkg cream cheese

Cream butter and cream cheese. Add flour, refrigerate 1 hour. Form into 24 small balls and press into small muffin tins.

FILLING:

¾ c brown sugar   1 tsp vanilla extract
1 egg, well beaten   Pinch of salt
1 tbsp butter, melted   ¾ to 1 c pecans, chopped

Pour filling mixture into shells. Bake at 350° for 25 minutes.

Bon-Bon Christmas Cookies

4 oz cream cheese
½ c butter-flavored shortening
2 c flour, sifted

1½ c confectioners' sugar, sifted
2 10-oz jars maraschino
   cherries, drained

In a medium bowl, stir together cream cheese and shortening until well blended. Stir in flour, using your hands, if needed, to help it form a dough. If mixture seems too dry, add a couple of teaspoons of water. Cover and chill several hours or overnight.

Preheat oven to 375°. Lightly grease cookie sheets. Before rolling out dough, dust rolling surface heavily with confectioners' sugar. Roll dough out to $\frac{1}{8}$-inch thickness. Cut into 1x4-inch strips. Place a cherry on end of each strip. Roll up each strip starting with the cherry. Place on prepared cookie sheets and dust with a little confectioners' sugar. Bake for 7 to 10 minutes in preheated oven. Cookies should brown slightly. Dust again with confectioners' sugar. Allow cookies to cool before serving, as cherries are very hot!

Christmas Logs

8 c flour
1 (¼-oz) pkg active dry yeast
2 c butter or margarine
3 egg yolks
1 egg
2 c heavy whipping cream
1 tsp salt

1 tbsp vanilla extract
3 egg whites
4 c walnuts, ground
1⅓ c sugar
2 tbsp ground cinnamon
2 tbsp bread crumbs, dried
Sugar (for sprinkling)

Combine flour, yeast, and butter or margarine by hand until mixture is crumbly. Stir in egg yolks, egg, heavy cream, salt, and vanilla. Mix together and let stand in refrigerator for 8 hours or overnight.

Beat egg whites until stiff peaks are formed. In a separate bowl, mix walnuts, sugar, cinnamon, and bread crumbs. Stir in egg whites and let filling stand for 1 hour.

Divide dough into fourths. On a surface sprinkled with white sugar, roll ¼ of dough out very thin (you should be almost able to see through the dough.) into a rectangular or square shape. Spread ¼ of the filling over rolled dough. Cut dough into 2½x2½-inch squares. Roll each square up like a jelly roll and place on a baking sheet. Repeat with remaining dough and filling. Keep dough you aren't working with in refrigerator. Bake at 350° for 20 minutes. Keep a close eye on these cookies as they tend to burn easily because of the sugar coating.

Holly Berry Cookies

2 c flour
1 c sugar
1 tsp ground cinnamon
$\frac{3}{4}$ tsp baking powder
$\frac{1}{4}$ tsp salt
$\frac{1}{2}$ c butter, chilled
1 egg

$\frac{1}{4}$ c milk
$\frac{2}{3}$ c seedless raspberry jam
2 c confectioners' sugar
2 tbsp milk
$\frac{1}{2}$ tsp vanilla extract
$\frac{1}{4}$ c cinnamon red hot candies
4 drops green food coloring

In a large bowl combine flour, sugar, ground cinnamon, baking powder, and salt. Cut in butter until mixture resembles coarse crumbs. In a small bowl, beat egg and $\frac{1}{4}$ cup milk. Add to crumb mixture until dough is moistened. Cover and refrigerate for at least 1 hour.

Preheat oven to 375°. On a lightly floured surface, roll out dough to $\frac{1}{8}$ inch thick. Cut with a 2-inch round cookie cutter. Place on ungreased baking sheets. Bake for 8–10 minutes or until edges are lightly browned. Cool on wire racks. Once cool, spread jam on half of the cookies, then top each with another cookie.

GLAZE:

Combine confectioners' sugar, 2 tablespoons milk, and vanilla until smooth. Spread glaze over cookie and decorate with red cinnamon candy before glaze is set. Let dry. Using a small, new paintbrush and green food coloring, paint holly leaves on cookies.

Fruit Foldovers

2 c flour
¼ c sugar
⅛ tsp salt
1 8-oz pkg cream cheese
1 c butter

1 c crushed pineapple
    pie filling
1 c confectioners' sugar
½ tsp rum-flavored extract
1½ tbsp water
2 tsp light corn syrup

In a large bowl, mix flour, sugar, and salt. Cut in cream cheese and butter until mixture resembles coarse crumbs. Work dough with hands until it holds together. Divide dough into four balls, wrap in waxed paper, and refrigerate for 2 hours or until dough is firm.

On a lightly floured surface, roll one of the dough balls into a 10-inch circle. Use a 3-inch cutter to cut dough into circles. Place ½ teaspoon of pie filling in center of each circle. Moisten edge of dough and fold over. Seal edge by pressing with the tines of a fork dipped in flour. Place on an ungreased baking sheet. Repeat with remaining dough. Bake at 350° for 20 to 25 minutes or until golden brown. Once cool, drizzle with glaze.

GLAZE:

Combine confectioners' sugar, rum flavoring, water, and corn syrup. Mix until smooth. Keep covered until ready to use.

Plum Jam Cookies

8 oz butter
1 c brown sugar, packed
1 egg
¼ c water

3 c flour
1 pinch salt
1 tsp baking powder
1 c plum (or any other flavor) jam

In a large bowl, cream together butter and brown sugar. Beat in egg and water. Sift together flour, salt, and baking powder; stir into butter mixture until well blended. On a lightly floured surface, roll out dough to ¼-inch thickness. Cut with a 2-inch round cookie cutter. Put half of the cookies onto a cookie sheet and spread ½ teaspoon of plum jam in center of each one. With a thimble, or small cookie cutter, cut center out of remaining cookies. Place these on top of jam-topped cookies to make sandwiches. Press together. Bake cookies at 375° for 10 minutes, then remove to a rack to cool.

Orange Shortbread Fingers

³/₄ c flour   1 orange peel, grated
3 tbsp cornstarch   ¼ tsp salt
¼ c plus 2 tbsp sugar   7 tbsp unsalted butter, chopped

Preheat oven to 300°. Grease an 8-inch square pan. Into a medium bowl, sift flour and cornstarch. Add ¼ cup sugar, orange peel, and salt.

Using your fingertips, work butter into dry ingredients until mixture resembles fine crumbs. Knead mixture until it forms a dough, then press it into prepared pan. Score dough into 24 narrow rectangles and prick with the tines of a fork. Sprinkle with 2 tablespoons of sugar. Bake for 30 minutes or until a pale golden color. Remove from oven and leave shortbread to cool in pan until it holds its shape enough to turn out on a rack. When completely cooled, cut shortbread into fingers along the scored lines. The cookies can be stored in an airtight container for up to 1 week.

Gingerbread People

4 c flour, sifted
1 tbsp ground cinnamon
2 tsp baking powder
1½ tsp ground ginger
1½ tsp ground cloves
1 tsp baking soda
1 tsp ground nutmeg

1 tsp salt
1 c unsalted butter (not
    margarine), room
    temperature
1 c sugar
2 large eggs, separated
1 c molasses
1 tbsp cold water

OPTIONAL DECORATIONS:

Currants for eyes
Strips of candied cherries for
    smiles

Red hot cinnamon candies
    for buttons

2½ c confectioners' sugar, sifted   3–4 tbsp cold water
½ tsp vanilla extract   Assorted food colors

Onto a piece of waxed paper, sift 3¾ cups flour, cinnamon, baking powder, ginger, cloves, baking soda, nutmeg, and salt. In a large bowl, with an electric mixer on high, cream butter and sugar until light yellow and fluffy. Beat in egg yolks, one at a time, then molasses. Using a wooden spoon, stir in flour mixture. Cover and refrigerate dough for at least 1 hour or overnight.

Preheat oven to 350°. Butter three baking sheets. On a pastry cloth or board, sprinkle remaining ¼ cup flour and roll out half of the dough, ¼ inch thick. With cookie cutters, cut out gingerbread people. With a spatula, transfer them back to baking sheets. Decorate with currants, cherries, and cinnamon candies if you wish. In a cup, whisk egg whites with water. Bake cookies for 5 minutes, then brush lightly with egg white mixture. Bake 2 to 3 minutes more. Let cool on baking sheets for 2 minutes. (To make holes for hanging, pierce top of each cookie with a skewer as soon as it comes out of the oven.) With a spatula, transfer to racks to cool. Repeat with remaining dough and flour.

To Make Icing:

In a small bowl, stir sugar with vanilla, then add enough water to make a stiff icing. Divide into small cups and color as you wish. When cookies are cold, pipe out designs, such as smiling faces, zigzags, bow ties, and aprons. If using different colors of icing, let one color dry before piping next. Store cookies in an airtight container for up to 2 weeks. Do not freeze, as icing could crack.

Surprise Packages

1 c butter	3 c flour
1 c sugar	1 tsp baking soda
½ c brown sugar	¼ tsp salt
2 eggs	48 thin-layered chocolate
1 tsp vanilla extract	mint wafers

Cream butter and sugars until light and fluffy. Beat in eggs and vanilla. In a separate bowl, combine dry ingredients. Gradually add to creamed mixture. Mix well. Divide dough in half; wrap each in plastic wrap and refrigerate 1 to 2 hours. Preheat oven to 375°. Work with ½ the dough at a time. Using a scant tablespoon of dough, cover each mint, forming a rectangular shaped cookie. Bake 10 to 12 minutes. Cool. Can be decorated with icing to look like a wrapped package.

No-Bake Sweets

*"Who then is the faithful and wise servant,
whom the master has put in charge of the servants
in his household to give them their food at the proper time?"*

MATTHEW 24:45

Cherry Surprises

½ c butter, softened
1¾ c confectioners' sugar
1 tsp orange juice

1½ c coconut, shredded
1 10-oz jar maraschino cherries,
    drained

In a medium bowl, cream together butter, confectioners' sugar, and orange juice; mix in coconut. Wrap coconut mixture around each cherry to cover completely. Store in refrigerator in a tightly covered container until ready to serve.

Peanut Butter Balls

½ c peanut butter
½ c honey or corn syrup
¾ c nonfat dry milk

1 c crispy cereal flakes
Coconut or chopped nuts

Mix peanut butter and honey or corn syrup in a bowl. Stir in dry milk. Stir in cereal. Roll mixture into ¾-inch balls. Roll balls in coconut or nuts. Put into a container and store in refrigerator.

Swedish No-Bake Chocolate Balls

3 sticks margarine
2 c sugar
3 tbsp dark coffee (liquid)
3 tbsp cocoa

3 tsp vanilla extract
5 c quick oats
Coconut and colored sprinkles

Mix all ingredients in a bowl and form into ¾-inch balls. Dip in coconut and colored sprinkles. Refrigerate.

Christmas Orange Balls ʃ

4 c graham cracker crumbs
1 c confectioners' sugar
1 c pecans, chopped
¼ c light corn syrup

1 6-oz can frozen orange juice
   concentrate, thawed
¼ c butter, melted
⅓ c confectioners' sugar

In a medium bowl, stir together graham cracker crumbs, 1 cup confectioners' sugar, and pecans. Make a well in center and pour in corn syrup, orange juice concentrate, and melted butter. Mix well by hand until dough forms. Roll into 1-inch balls and roll balls in confectioners' sugar. Store at room temperature in an airtight container. Put a sheet of waxed paper between layers to prevent sticking.

Easy 5-in-1 No-Bake Cookies

BASE:

½ c peanut butter
½ c honey or corn syrup

¼ c orange juice concentrate
1½ c nonfat dry milk

Mix thoroughly. Now choose one of the following 5 steps:

OATMEAL RAISIN:

2 c rolled oats   1½ c raisins

Mix into base. Shape into balls, then flatten.

CRISPY BALLS:

4 c crispy cereal

Mix into base. Shape into small balls.

RAISIN CLUSTERS:

¼ c cocoa   4 c raisins

Mix into base. Form into small balls.

COCOA BALLS:

¼ c cocoa
2 c rolled oats

¼ c peanuts, chopped
1 tsp vanilla extract

Mix into base. Shape into balls.

GRAHAMIES:

¼ c raisins

Mix into base. Spread between graham crackers.

Peanut Butter Snacks

1 3-oz can Chinese noodles
1 c miniature marshmallows

1 6-oz pkg butterscotch chips
½ c peanut butter

Put noodles and marshmallows into large mixing bowl. Tear 2 large pieces of aluminum foil and lay on flat surface. Melt chips and peanut butter in double boiler over boiling water or in heavy pan. Stir until smooth. Pour mixture over Chinese noodles and marshmallows and mix (like popcorn balls). Spoon out by tablespoonfuls onto foil. Cool in refrigerator until hard.

No-Bake Peanut Butter Bars

2 c graham cracker crumbs	1 lb confectioners' sugar
2 c peanut butter	½ lb margarine or butter

Combine in mixing bowl and spread in ungreased 9x13-inch pan. Prepare frosting as follows.

FROSTING:

¼ c margarine   6 oz semisweet chocolate chips

Melt together. Spread over bars. Refrigerate; cut into squares.

Chocolate-Covered Orange Balls

1 lb confectioners' sugar
1 12-oz pkg vanilla
   wafers, crushed
1 c walnuts, chopped

¼ lb butter
1 6-oz can frozen orange
   juice concentrate, thawed
1½ lb milk chocolate, melted

In a large bowl, combine confectioners' sugar, vanilla wafers, walnuts, butter, and orange juice. Mix well and shape into 1-inch round balls; allow to dry for 1 hour. Place chocolate chips in top of double boiler. Stir frequently over medium heat until melted. Dip balls into melted chocolate and place in decorative paper cups.

No-Bake Peanut Oatmeal Drops

1 c sugar
¼ c butter
⅓ c evaporated milk
1 c peanut butter

½ tsp vanilla extract
1 c rolled oats
½ c peanuts

Bring sugar, butter, and milk to a rolling boil. Boil for 3 minutes, stirring frequently. Remove from heat and stir in peanut butter, vanilla, rolled oats, and peanuts. Drop by teaspoonfuls onto waxed paper. Let stand until set.

Chocolate Balls

1 c peanut butter
¾ c confectioners' sugar
1 c graham cracker crumbs
2 c semisweet chocolate chips

3 1-oz squares semisweet
  chocolate, chopped
1 tbsp shortening

In a medium bowl, mix together peanut butter and confectioners' sugar until smooth. Stir in graham cracker crumbs until well blended. Form dough into 1-inch balls by rolling in your hands, or by using a cookie scoop. Melt semisweet chocolate chips, semisweet chocolate squares, and shortening in top half of a double boiler. Use a fork to dip balls into melted chocolate, and place on waxed paper to cool until set.

No-Bake Chocolate Peanut Butter Oatmeal Cookies

2 tbsp butter
¼ c cocoa
½ c sugar
¼ c milk (condensed or whole milk)
Dash salt

1 tsp vanilla extract
1 heaping tbsp peanut butter
(add more to taste and
increase oatmeal)
1½ c uncooked oatmeal

Microwave butter in a microwave-safe bowl for 15–30 seconds, until butter is melted. Add cocoa and blend until cocoa is dissolved into butter. Add sugar, milk, and salt. Blend well. Microwave on high for 1 minute, 10 seconds to bring to a full boil. (Should you need to microwave batter some more, do so in 10-second increments. You want a full boil, but it will continue to cook after it's removed from microwave. Heating too long can cause mixture to scorch.) Add vanilla, peanut butter, and oatmeal. Stir well. Drop by tablespoonfuls onto waxed paper and allow to cool.

Fun Christmas Sweets to Make or Give Away

Through Jesus, therefore,
let us continually offer to God a sacrifice of praise—
the fruit of lips that confess his name.
And do not forget to do good and to share with others,
for with such sacrifices God is pleased.

HEBREWS 13:15–16

Cookie Jar Sugar Cookies

4 c flour	½ tsp salt
1 tsp baking powder	¾ tsp ground nutmeg
½ tsp baking soda	1½ c sugar

Combine flour with baking powder, baking soda, salt, and nutmeg. In a clean 1-liter glass jar with a wide mouth, layer sugar followed by flour mixture. Press firmly in place and seal. Attach a card with the following instructions:

Sugar Cookies

In a large bowl, beat 1 egg with 1 cup softened butter or margarine until light and fluffy. At low speed of an electric mixer, add ½ cup sour cream, 1 teaspoon vanilla, and contents of jar. Mix until combined, using hands if necessary. Cover dough and refrigerate for several hours or overnight. Remove dough from refrigerator. Preheat oven to 375°. Roll chilled dough out on a lightly floured surface to ⅛ inch thick. Cut dough into desired shapes. Place on an ungreased cookie sheet and bake for 10 to 12 minutes.

Chocolate Chip Cookie Mix in a Jar

1 tsp salt
1 tsp baking soda
2 c flour

1 c brown sugar, packed
½ c sugar
1½ c semisweet chocolate chips

Mix salt and baking soda with flour, then layer remaining ingredients into a 1-quart, wide-mouth jar. Use scissors to cut a 9-inch circle from calico. Place over lid, and secure with rubber band. Tie on a raffia or ribbon bow to cover rubber band. Enclose a card with the following mixing and baking directions:

Chocolate Chip Cookies

Preheat oven to 375°. In a large bowl, cream 1 cup of unsalted butter or margarine until light and fluffy. Beat in 1 egg and 1 teaspoon of vanilla. Mix in cookie mix. Drop teaspoonfuls of dough, spaced well apart, onto a greased cookie sheet. Bake for 8 to 10 minutes in preheated oven, or until lightly browned. Cool on wire racks.

Oatmeal Raisin Spice Cookie Mix in a Jar

1 c flour
1 tsp ground cinnamon
½ tsp ground nutmeg
1 tsp baking soda
½ tsp salt

¾ c raisins
2 c rolled oats
¾ c brown sugar, packed
½ c sugar

Mix together flour, ground cinnamon, ground nutmeg, baking soda, and salt. Set aside. Layer ingredients in the following order into a 1-quart, wide-mouth jar: flour mixture, raisins, rolled oats, brown sugar, and sugar. Firmly pack down each layer before adding next layer. Attach a tag with the following instructions:

Oatmeal Raisin Spice Cookies

Preheat oven to 350°. Line cookie sheets with parchment paper. Empty jar of cookie mix into large mixing bowl. Add ³/₄ cup butter or margarine, softened. Stir in 1 slightly beaten egg and 1 teaspoon of vanilla. Mix until combined, using hands if necessary. Shape into balls the size of walnuts. Place on lined cookie sheets 2 inches apart. Bake for 11 to 13 minutes in preheated oven, or until edges are lightly browned. Cool 5 minutes on cookie sheet. Transfer cookies to wire racks to finish cooling.

Chocolate Chip Walnut Cookie Mix in a Jar

1 c flour
½ tsp baking powder
½ tsp baking soda
1¼ c rolled oats
1 1½-oz bar milk chocolate

½ c sugar
½ c brown sugar, packed
½ c walnuts, chopped
½ c semisweet chocolate chips

Use a funnel that has a 2-inch opening to layer nicely in jar. With wire whisk, mix flour, baking powder, and baking soda. Pour into jar; pack down level with heavy object. Mix oatmeal in a blender. Grate chocolate bar, and mix into oatmeal. Pack on top of flour in jar. Add white sugar and pack down. Add brown sugar and pack down. Layer chopped nuts on top of

154

brown sugar. Finish layering jar with mini or regular chocolate chips until even with the top (no more than ½ cup). Enclose a card with the following mixing and baking directions:

Chocolate Chip Walnut Cookies

Preheat oven to 375°. Spoon chocolate chips and nuts into small bowl; set aside. Spoon sugars into mixing bowl; add ½ cup margarine or butter, cream well. Add 1 egg and ½ teaspoon vanilla; mix well. Pour oatmeal and flour mixture from jar into bowl and mix thoroughly. Stir in chocolate chips and nuts. Roll into walnut-size balls; place on slightly greased cookie sheet 2 inches apart. Bake for 8 to 10 minutes.

Brownie Mix in a Jar

1¼ c flour
1 tsp baking powder
1 tsp salt

⅔ c cocoa powder, unsweetened
2¼ c sugar
½ c pecans, chopped

Mix together flour, baking powder, and salt in a quart jar. Layer remaining ingredients in the order listed. Press each layer firmly in place before adding next layer. Wipe out the inside of jar with a dry paper towel after adding cocoa powder, so other layers will show through the glass. Attach a tag with the following instructions:

Brownies

Preheat oven to 350°. Grease and flour a 9x13-inch baking pan. Empty jar of brownie mix into a large mixing bowl, and stir to blend. Mix in ¾ cup melted butter and 4 eggs. Mix thoroughly. Spread batter evenly into prepared baking pan. Bake for 25 to 30 minutes in preheated oven. Cool completely in pan before cutting into 2-inch squares.

Butterscotch Brownies

2 c flour
1½ tbsp baking powder
¼ tsp salt

½ c coconut, flaked
¾ c pecans, chopped
2 c brown sugar, packed

To a 1-liter jar, add flour, baking powder, and salt; stir together, and pack down. Then add and pack down remaining ingredients in this order: coconut, pecans, brown sugar. Attach a label with the following instructions:

Butterscotch Brownies

Preheat oven to 375°. Grease a 9x13-inch baking pan. Empty jar of brownie mix into a large mixing bowl; stir to break up lumps. Add ¾ cup softened butter, 2 beaten eggs, and 2 teaspoons of vanilla extract; mix until well blended. Spread batter evenly in prepared pan. Bake for 25 minutes. Allow to cool in pan before cutting into squares.

Be joyful in hope,
patient in affliction,
faithful in prayer.
Share with God's people who are in need.
Practice hospitality.

Romans 12:12–13